I0510910

Congratulation!
You are jobless

Congratulation!
You are jobless

Conquering The Unemployed Evil

NIRANJAN KUMAR

First Edition: 2017

Second Edition: 2019

Copyright © Niranjan kumar 2017 2019

Email: niruniranjan.kumar07@gmail.com

www.facebook.com/niranjan.kumar.90663894

Dedicated To

A Special Dedication to all the jobless

This book is dedicated to my

Father, **Rambilas Singh**
Mother, **Kunti Devi**
Wife, **Swati Singh**
Nephew, **Darsh Suman**

About This Book

This is a self-help book for unemployed people. Actually, being a jobless is more than what we and our society interpret. Unemployment is a bridging path between the harsh realities and the brightest of possibilities.

Different parts of this book bring their own flavor. The very first part, *"Through the Realities"* explains the facts with research data associated to the unemployment on global upfront. They are needed to know because, to conquer an enemy we have to know the enemy from inside out.

The second part *"The Psychology Of Jobless minds"* will unleash how and what different unemployed people think and respond to the state of being jobless.

The third part *"Congratulation, You Are Jobless"* is actually the core of this book. Through this part you will learn what's good in being a jobless? Why and how to live life on your terms? And some of the best success stories of jobless people who made it large when they were down and out.

The last part *"Learning The Lessons"*, teaches different lessons, tips needed when you are jobless and life seems a burden. Example – How to enjoy life being jobless? How to stay motivated? & more.

About The Author

The author of this book, Niranjan Kumar is a self-publishing author; an educator by nature & an entrepreneur by passion who loves to educate, motivate & help out a needy one.

He holds Bachelor of Engineering (BE) degree in Electronics and Telecommunication from RTMNU, Maharashtra, India. & Master of Technology (M.Tech) degree in VLSI from RGPV, Madhya Pradesh, India..

There are two research papers in international journals to his name. Readers can contact him through …

www.facebook.com/niranjan.kumar.90663894

Email: niruniranjan.kumar07@gmail.com

Acknowledgement

Gratitude is the best way to appreciate anyone's contribution. Every work gets accomplished successfully through many characters behind the scene. This book too is no different. There's whole a list of people who stood by me throughout the work. To begin with I would like to express my deep sense of gratitude to my elder sister - *Pratibha Suman*, wife - *Swati Singh* who kept me motivated whenever I felt down & under whose able guidance this book saw the light of the day. I will also be ever indebted to my brother Ranjan Suman for support, morale boosting and encouragement.

It will be unfair to miss the contributions of my friends especially *Abhishek Kumar & Sandeep Sharma* whose honest feedbacks helped a lot and other family members, who has been supportive throughout to keep me motivated.

I also beg forgiveness to everyone whose names I just missed to mention. You all are equally deserving. Thank you all!

A Note To My Lovely Readers

Firstly, I'm grateful to you for picking this book. Just to make you read this book in a guided way, I make an appeal related to content of the book.

I request you while reading this book, if you readers want to skip initial parts of this book you can but, **must not give a miss to Part 3 & Part 4**. *I promise these two parts will surely going to be filled with transformational rich contents. You can happily give a miss to Part 1 and some portion of Part 2 as part 1 is full of contents that will only support to clear your understanding the purpose and existence of this book.*

Here's, my ratings for the level of importance of this book by parts.

Part 1	★ ★
Part 2	☆ ☆ ☆
Part 3	★ ★ ★ ★ ★
Part 4	☆ ☆ ☆ ☆

What's Inside

Part 1 - Through the Realities

Part 2 - The Psychology of Jobless Minds

Part 3 - Congratulation!You are Jobless

Part 4 - Learning the Lessons

PART 1

Through The Realities

"An unemployed existence is a worse negation of life than death itself."

- José Ortega y Gasset

CHAPTER 1

No Rosy Picture In Reality

No Rosy Picture
In Reality

We are in the age, which is being largely dominated by Super computers, Smart phones, Digital Medias and eye popping inventions. Human resource is getting replaced by machines. Lives seem too reliant on internet and capsules. We hunt our identity, happiness, opportunities and success formula on internet. Consumption graph of sleeping pills is rising. While a part of our population still holding textbooks, living comfortably at home, going school without any real stress, enjoying holidays with family and friends, counting their age and waiting for their turn to advance into the world of some serious stress, despair, depression, rejection, humiliation, considerable amount of opportunities and success.

Well, there is another fraction of the population who has already marched into the thick of things. Feeling strangled, raising a question mark over their existence and quite a few of them somehow trying to hang in there. In the wake of it, the unemployment issue is becoming a hot potato throughout the world. Some will accept it and some will deny. But, at the end of the day we have to believe it either being a parent or as a jobless individual.

Forget the present scenario; going by the research it doesn't seem to paint a rosy picture, at least for couple of more years from now. A research conducted by International Labor Organization (ILO) predicts that joblessness will surpass 200 million by the end of 2017. To be more precise, it's been revealed that more than 3 million will be unemployed worldwide in the next two years. According to them this will be largely due to the economic slowdown. But, only economic slowdown can't be blamed for such a huge number of rising joblessness. There are certain other dynamics that are responsible too. If we enlist all of them individually, then they will be in numbers.

I strongly believe that all the causes, consequences and solutions related to joblessness are concealed within the types of unemployment. Problems itself have a solution, right? What we need is to just open our eye, accept the reality and shift our focus towards possible opportunities. But, as I said earlier we will focus and discuss it latter humorously, how to enjoy being jobless? So, again shifting focus back on this very part, next we will get to know three major types of unemployment, which actually holds all the secrets of joblessness.

CHAPTER 2

Why Are You Jobless

Why Are You Jobless

While sitting all alone, after facing bad times every individual ask one question either to themselves or to their destiny – Why me?

You may have asked the same when got punched through the phase of rejection, sour experiences and being labeled as good for nothing. I heard people answering that all this has to do with downtrodden economy. But, is this the only reason? No. You too have to take responsibility. Don't play the blame game, always. Although, the types of unemployment discussed will clear picture in wider frame, here are some reasons of why are you jobless on personal echelon. Yeah, I understand that many of you may not find more of the something new here but, it indeed will be reminder for many of you to know some good reasons to not cracking a job interview, though it's not the primary concern of this book to train you for a job selection. Here it goes!

Apathetic Demeanor: What the hell !

A man with a laid back demeanor and who does not considers his work important is frequently thought to be apathetic. On the off chance that you stroll in a meeting with a laid back and conceited mentality, the chance is very high that you won't get up with the employment and your interviewer will not make any delay to kick your ass out of the door. So ensure that you indicate excitement about the organization.

Your Resume Kills You

Your resume should just comprise of subtle elements which are precise and brief. A long and protracted resume with a considerable measure of language is the first to arrive up in the trash canister. Additionally it is essential to edit the resume and redress all the unnoticed blunders and grammatical errors. Keep in mind, your resume is the primary snippet of information that you convey. It should be flawless and to the point.

If you present certain interests in your resume and while interviewing you say something that seems contradictory. The employer will perceive you as the 'utter confused' having no structured thoughts. Employer will build a perception that you are unable to handle pressure and this might go against you.

You are blurred about the job

Absence of enthusiasm for the working of the firm and not willing to find out about the procedures of how the organization work are a part of the things that symbolize your absence of intrigue. It squanders the employer's time as well as yours. The interviewers are entirely savvy with regards to judging the behavioral patterns of individuals particularly the individuals whom they are interviewing. So, in the process they can clearly notice that you are unclear about the job that will surely result in you being rejected.

You are grown up now, don't be a kid

Most commonly when you go for a job interview straight after college days it could become apparent to hiring manager that you are still in your college days. Nobody would like to hire a kid. When it's time to grow up one should, especially during job interviews. You will be kicked if you are stuck having one foot in college and another in the real world. So it is the high time to bid adieu to recklessness and start preparing for becoming a responsible and whole new transformed individual.

Your communication skill is flat and dead

Have you noticed almost every job opportunity offered have common criteria of having good communication skills? A curious face has a body language which describes all of these qualities. Interview is the first and the foremost test that explains your behavioral and psychological traits to the interviewer. If you do not know how to talk or behave in a certain way that is required in the formal world, there is a high possibility of you being asked to leave the door.

Your best appearance is the formal one

It is vital to look formal and very much mannered while going for an interview. Stubble and tousled hair won't just influence you to resemble a disorderly individual in addition to this the interviewer will think that you are not genuine about the job. So it is constantly better to have a polished and respectable look which will influence the interviewer to like your appearance. It is likewise critical to dress in formals while going for an interview. Formal attire gives a solid perception in the psyches of the interviewer.

You are not making new connections

In modern world is a digital one. People are connected through various social platforms but mostly for entertainment. People are not taking full and real advantage of it. When it comes to job search you should use these digital platforms to reach out to right people at all times. No networking means you are deprived of certain job prospective. Networking has helped much land dream jobs which was a win-win situation for the employees as well as the company. So it's time to get networking savvy and make complete use of the internet and its boons.

You are a spoiled brat

Your life was not intervened with financial or other needs until you got out of your college and began to look for a job. Till now you were served everything right in your plate. But now you have to fetch them all by yourself. However, if you enter an employer's cabin with an 'I'm daddy's or momma's boy attitude' you could be mistaken as an entirely dependent identity. Your chances of getting the job will come down to almost zero. So, it's time to pull up your shocks and stand up on your own.

You are a liar

Even a liar himself wants to have a person who always speaks the truth. Every company needs honest and loyal employees who will honestly put in all the effort to give their best for the company. An imposter will never be liked by anyone. If you are not so, you will be dumped by your employer. Even if you received the job you will be fired soon no matter how qualified you are.

Your deformed personality traits

Dull & Depressed: You can be depressed with anything be it you got laid off by previous organization, not getting any job after a number of attempts or your girlfriend dumped you; You must not present yourself dull and depressed. A professional people must know how to deal with personal problems without cribbing. The company has nothing to do with your personal problems. A weepy face will only piss off your employer. You will be perceived as naive and immature for spilling your problems in front of strangers. Companies want people who know how to keep their personal and professional life separate. .

Greedy: Fresher or people with a lesser experience should not bombard the interviewers with their expectations and wishes as they may consider it as rude and nonchalant.

Your lavish desire and expectations propel you to fix the price of your services. You should understand that you don't have liberty to finalize your salary specially being inexperienced. If this is the case then its better you should stay at home and watch TV. Never be greedy when it comes to jobs. It is always better to take whatever they give especially if you are a fresher. With the number of applicants increasing it is difficult to find the perfect jobs with all the perks.

You may be on the receiving end of monthly bonuses or generous gift vouchers in your last job but you do not need to tell this to your interviewer. On the day of the interview if you keep telling them about the perks and bonuses that you are expecting to receive, you should, might as well wave a good bye to the job.

Jack of all trades but the master of none

It could be possible that you have the knowledge of numerous topics but not having excellence in any of the particular topics. The fact that you know every topic can grab the eyeballs only but not the opportunity. While choosing a profession it is important to be clear about the goals and it is a need to absorb as much knowledge about the particular subject. It is always better to have a master than the jack in every corporation.

Beating around the bush

Employer asks you some real good and important question to know how seriously you have taken the consideration of joining the firm and in reply you beat around the bush just to pretend you the answers. If the person beats around the bush and tries to dodge various questions, he is most certainly thought of as a person who will run from his responsibilities and give excuses time and again.

You are unprepared or underprepared

Maximum number of people doesn't feel it important to know the organization and research how it works before going for an interview. You should be prepared for the questions that will be thrown at you. Otherwise, it's better to miss the interview. It is a waste of your as well as the interviewers time. With many other candidates who are highly prepared as well as very much qualified, you will have no chance in bagging the job that you have been 'waiting' for.

You are evasive: Don't be a parrot

Don't act like a parrot i.e to vomit whatever you know irrespective of what got asked. When asked about certain trick questions it is important to be honest rather than just rattling out the million times used answers. If you are asked about your weaknesses it is better if you are honest and tell the interviewer a couple of them rather than acting like you are flawless. Interviewers are smart enough to not give in on such evasiveness.

You don't have the skill and the knowledge

One of the things that irk interviewers the most is people who come for interviews who are not even remotely qualified for the job. They don't have the required skills and knowledge to excel in that particular job. Lays you off in front of potential bosses as there might be other vacancies in the same company in which you have applied in the future.

You are low on confidence

Interviewer will certainly put you in a spot of bother and squeeze your brain just to know how confident you are. Lack of confidence is a non tolerant trait in any employee and this will surely keep you unemployed.

Now, we will discuss the types of unemployment which will reveal why an individual failing to get a job. These are beyond personal. Taking into account various aspects of unemployment in an economy, it is majorly categorized into three types. These are Structural, Frictional and Cyclical. As these are vindicated briefly:

Structural Unemployment

When a labor market fail to provide jobs for everyone who is seeking job then structural unemployment is said to be occurred. It can be made clear by the fact that actually it arises due to mismatch between skills required for a job and skills available for the job. However, it also gets affected at times by cyclical

Unemployment. *For example-* consider that recession is going on for engineers. Actually it's a fact. There is indeed a recession in technical job sector. And chances looks gloomy that it is going to last any time soon. So imagine you have a particular skill which actually required currently but you are not getting your chance right now for some reasons. After a long period when recession will end there are chances that the individual skills you had then are now obsolete. Employers don't need you now. For the new comer there will be opportunities. But for you, still there will be the same scenario. Yes, having said that, you have only chance if you have developed a new skill during the period of being jobless.

Frictional Unemployment

Frictional unemployment is going to persist forever. Only change associated with it is its degree of effects. Because, it is mainly caused when a worker is searching or shifting from one job to another. The time frame during which he has no job comes under frictional unemployment. Reasons for shifting among jobs may be varied. For example – friction between a worker and employer, a worker not enjoying the current job, discontent due to skills, payment, work time, location, seasonal jobs, attitude and other factors.

Cyclical Unemployment

This type of unemployment causes if there is not much demand to provide a job for everyone who is willing to work, due to the varying nature of economy. This can also be named as *recession*. If there is less production needed, it is quite obvious that less work force will require. Hence, results into increased number of unemployed and decreased job vacancies.

CHAPTER 3

Deep Into The Realities

3

Deep Into The Realities

Raymond Torres, one of the report's author said that expected result of surpassing 200 million joblessness by the end of 2017 was supported with increasing insecurity, as solid jobs are replaced by unstable work in developing and developed countries. Means those who already have a job are not quite sure about their future. They have a sense of insecurity. Insecurity of either they will be fired or they have to face the hit of sliced wages. Low wages can also lead to call it a day for few of them. However, ILO research also suggests that

UK is one of the stronger countries for employment. Britain's unemployment rate of 5.2% in October 2015 was the lowest since January 2006. Now, some of you might get animated knowing the fact, oh, wow I am going to book my flight ticket right now, Will land up straight in UK and start making tones of money or at least find a job that will pay more than average. Well, you are the boss of your imaginations and you are free to perceive whatever you want. I can't help it. But, you have to take account of all the parameters that affect you either positively or negatively. Viz. – current status, family support, your skills and your current mindset. You want the ball rolling on your feet, you have to fix all the parameters and make sure that things will fall in their place altogether.

Moreover, the data collected and believed by researcher are for their concern. As an unemployed person we look at those results quite differently. A jobless person look at it one dimensionally, an unemployed is unemployed as simple as that. They don't look much interested too peep into, why? I guess if we try to explore the reasons of unemployment, we will surely find many answers to how to get employed either working for someone else or getting self employed. And it is becoming the need of the hour that we ourselves do some introspection. However, we will discuss various strategies to get a good job in the following chapter as we are looking into the realities right in this chapter. It is required as this will help to understand the current scenario around us.

"Many working women and men are having to accept low paid jobs, both in emerging and developing economies, and also increasingly in developed countries. Despite a drop in the number of unemployed in some European countries and US, too many people are still jobless. We need to take urgent action to boost the number of descent work opportunities or we risk intensified social tensions" Said; Guy Ryder, the ILO director general.

Whatever the director general has said, it actually holds true in the sense that inability to produce sufficient job opportunities will create intensified social tensions. Actually, it all has already begun in some parts of the world. As an Indian citizen, at least I can assure of the very fact. If it consistently be able to advance for some more couple of years like this, I can guarantee you that there will be a virtual war among human kind for the sake of their own survival.

We exist in a world that clasps equal importance of every individual for the survival of the Homo sapiens. Be it's a doctor, an engineer, an accountant, a lawyer, a scientist, a shopkeeper, a servant and so on. It is indeed like very own ecosystem. As it's said, a balance is needed in the ecosystem to keep up the harmony. Either shortage or excess of a particular species will create turmoil and disrupt the harmony in the nature. Same is the case with our professional ecosystem. We

need to respect that. We can't say a priest, a

sweeper, or a servant should become obsolete. We need them equally. The irony is we ourselves are molding into a robot. And it is quite evident how the increasing number of robot depriving many of a job opportunities. We are now relying on machine more than human resource. It seems like our advancements are continuously into the world of mere caricatures. And, in this way we are becoming each other's enemy knowingly or unknowingly. Because, survival getting in danger.

As a latest research suggest that every year 45000 suicides happen worldwide due to unemployment. It is indeed true that economic slowdown has taken a hit on employment opportunities. But, researchers say that unemployment during good times or bad times is becoming a bigger factor in suicide than the economic catastrophe. World Health Organization (WHO) as per latest survey issued the research data and Sri Lanka topped it. I hope, at least you will never attempt suicide if you are an optimist. Instead of it, you will accept the reality and challenge the situations.

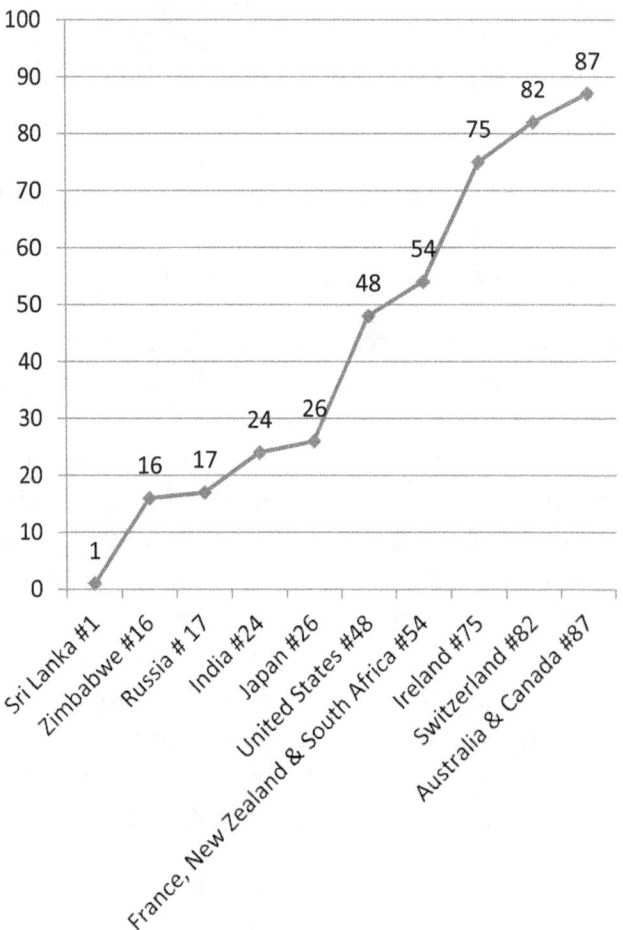

Well known countries that comes under 100 in suicide rate ranking (2015)

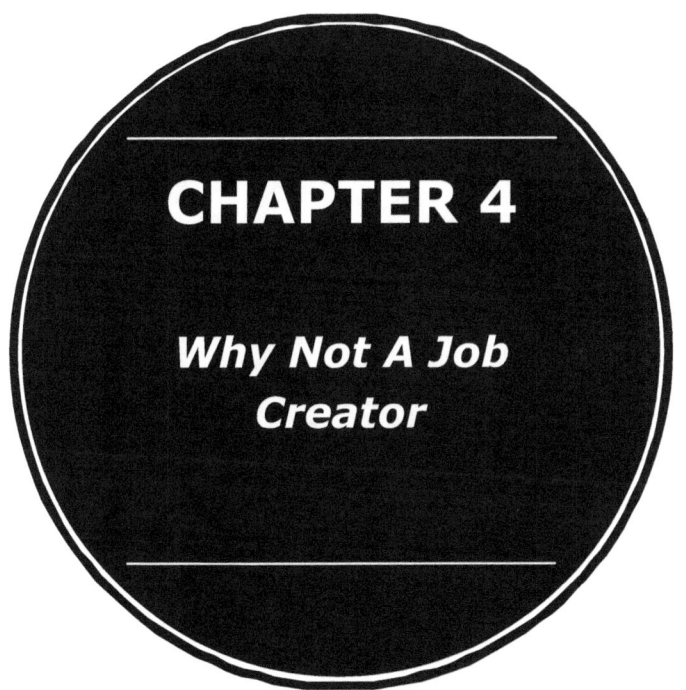

CHAPTER 4

Why Not A Job Creator

Why Not A Job Creator

"**T**he culture here is one of success based upon academic excellence, studying, learning, practicing and having a good job." – Said Steve Wozniak, Popularly known as Woz – The man who designed & engineered first home computer with keyboard & screen (Apple) along with his best friend- Steve Jobs.

This firm reply came from Woz when was asked - *If there's any possibility that any global tech giant can emerge from India?* Though, he don't know the Indian corporate culture deeply but, based upon his three times keynote experiences for One of the leading tech giant of India – Infosys, Woz collected that he just doesn't see any big advances coming out of tech companies in the likes of Infosys.

Considering the demography of Countries like India there's a lot of potential for executing fresh ideas and developing a culture of job creators but, nothing happening anything great off late. Though, lately it's been found that there is a sense of this culture flourishing. With this there is a constant rise in one alarming question – Why not a job creator? Well, the most basic answer to this is our mindset that built on beliefs of our surroundings & middle class culture. When I talk about the mindset then I talk about the two mindsets – One that's individual & the other is societal. The individual thought is indeed greatly driven by societal.

Talking about an individual's mind frame, a Jain philosopher – Jainacharya Ratnasunder Suri cited in one of his book about how the young generations heading towards becoming jobseekers & not the job creators. According to him young minds are trapped into the 1-2-3 program of multinational companies. What does it mean? It means *One* Individual – Getting salary of *two* people – By carrying work loads of *three*. Families are begging & breaking down into tears for love and personal attention that they are deprived of. The reason they are not thinking of an escape to this is the so called financial security & a little escape towards not getting challenged by following a fixed pattern of everyday routine. The Jain philosopher says that the people should break this psychological barrier by learning from a bird. Say, a parrot. Consider an employed person as a parrot in cage. The way a parrot gets food, security; personal attention & love all inside the cage, the very same way a person feel safe from challenges & receive financial support working under multinational companies. But, the real difference between parrot & a person holding a job is no matter what a parrot receive inside a cage there is always a desire to fly free but, it's not same with jobseekers. They look pretty amused with the fact that they don't have to face grueling challenges.

When it comes to societal mindset it's common that thinking of as a job creator instead of jobseeker thought of as a social crime. Middle class society can't see your dreams of becoming a writer like Shakespeare, painter like Pablo or philosopher like Socrates. They want you to be like others: work at a 9-5 job and make good money. They refuse to see the fact that not all engineers, MBA graduates and doctors who are making good money are happy with their jobs. There's not much support from middle class family and society. Right from our childhood people surrounding us tends to do our mental conditioning in a way as if the only purpose of education is to grab a job. Families look skeptical to infuse a thought process of an entrepreneur. Middle class perceive becoming a millionaire can only be possible through wrong deeds. Mentally downtrodden people of our society force an individual to make them believe that a millionaire or billionaire exists under different galaxy.

These thought process of people are not that suddenly infused in them; the root cause is generation carrying same thought process and transferring them to next generation over and over again. By chance, If someone gets inspired by any successful people who once belonged to the same place and they start believing in themselves then our family & society mark them as the biggest culprit as he/she has broken the rituals of a middle class thinking.

Does, not having a mindset of job creator is due to our mental conditioning only? Surely, not. People still find it cumbrous to enroll for entrepreneurial journey because of the risks involved, lack of leadership, the fighting spirit, lack of funding & more.

High Risk Factor: According to a survey, only one out of ten start-ups gets able to survive, rest of the 90% fail miserably. The high failure rate is mainly due to the risk factors directly involved in it in the likes of product risk, market risk, financial risk & execution risk. These risks can be summed up by launching right product to a demanding market with perfect execution plans that doesn't involve unbearable financial burden.

Lack of Leadership: Leadership qualities are something that a person carries within, if not, it can be developed through regular practices. When it comes to entrepreneurship, knack of leadership plays an undisputed role. Why someone finds entrepreneurship a hard nut to crack is because of the deficiency of leadership syndrome. A start-up is a rollercoaster ride that demand extra bit of responsibility from an individual. A leader must know to take strong & hard decisions and should be able to lead and guide his team in every situation. Someone might be great at their job but they find themselves claustrophobic when it comes to leading and delegating jobs.

Lack of Attitude: Looking at success of Paytm, Ola, Oyo, Airbnb & others people think entrepreneurship a cake walk. Soon they realize how tough & precarious it can be as they land their feet into it. Initially, when no one there is to believe you, it's only you who have to do every single bit of it. From researching - creating products & services - marketing efficiently & expensing smartly. When it seems bleak to garner result as per efforts and expectations our belief, emotions, & dream got shattered. And, then we all of a sudden decide to call it quit.

Lack of Funding: Although, lack of funds plays a great role in growing business thinking of its scalability, this should be the least important factor why people deviate from entrepreneurship. In few cases people decides to completely scrap business idea and stick to their job because of lack of investors or required sponsorships.

These challenges strongly fly in the face of the idea of becoming a job creator. The only way through this is having solid positive attitude towards problems. Your character being tested through all this & if you can conquer this surely there will be a better place for you to live for.

You try to stand still, polish your attitude, unlock your potentials & after initial hiccups, ultimately you will receive all the success present in the universe that jobseekers can only dream of.

PART 2

The Psychology

Of Jobless Minds

"A man willing to work, and unable to find work, is perhaps the saddest sight that fortune's inequality exhibits under this sun."

Thomas Carlyle

CHAPTER 1

From The Two
Unparallel Minds

1

From The Two Unparallel Minds

Being jobless is the worst feeling of all, isn't it? It becomes more torturous, more depressing, more frustrating and more heart breaking if you have the required qualification, required skills and individual talent. And, still you are not able to get through it. Getting no job for considerable periods still have some hopes associated but, if you are quite sure that there is big uncertainty over getting a job then it becomes almost impossible to hold on your spirit altogether and gather strength to fight the bad times. We apply for jobs, attend a number of interviews and get handed over rejection after rejection after rejection.

Being Jobless I've...

Humiliation, Desperation, Anger, Insecurity & more. BUT, not to forget the Freedom to do any wonder.

And if still we fail to find a work, most of us get a huge emotional as well as mental breakdown. We find ourselves caught up in darkness. Our chances of survival look gloomy. Countless negative thoughts come to our mind.

Ironically, the psychology of such minds is easy to read but difficult to find a solution out of it. Through this chapter we will find out, what a jobless mind thinks? How they respond to various situations?

Hi, Myself Abhay Jain, 28 years old. By the way, I must tell you, right now I am an entrepreneur. Just 3 years of experience.

Till my days at college I was like most of the other college guys. Charming, full of enthusiasm, having don't care attitude, confident, energetic and fun loving. I enjoyed a lot till my last official day of college life. Completed my engineering degree successfully in four years I had no plans for higher studies. A new leaf was to be turned now. Like all other parents my parent was also patiently looking at me, having a lot of expectations. So was the case with me. I was expecting a lot from myself as well. Quite confident till now, I was gearing up for job interviews. First couple of job interviews I was just overlooked. Reasons?- No experience. After few more attempts I thought someone has taken me a little seriously. But again got rejected, reason? I don't have skill that they were looking for. Previously, I was accepting my rejections as learning curve for me. But now, it began to take a toll on my mind. I kept looking for a job. And, got rejection after rejection. Ultimately, a breaking point came and I succumbed to it. And now I was officially a jobless. Wherever I went people asked the same question have you got any job? It looked more depressing when the same question- have your son found any job?, followed my parent everywhere. And my parent humiliation was spitting on my face. Your society will not let you go that easy if you are an unemployed. They have pretty much interest in what you are doing. And they will keep humiliating you. Well, that's the reality and can't be ignored very easily.

What I noticed and felt during the period of joblessness, going to summarize here:

Money directly proportional to love & respect: If you are not earning you will lose your respect. No one will respect you, neither your own family member including your parent nor the people of your society. They consider you good for nothing. You and your opinion will be ignored quite often.

You can't even think of your love life. Every girl will make a distance from you as soon as she will get to know you are jobless. It doesn't matter how good human being you are from heart or how good looking you are.

It becomes hard to be on social media: While I was jobless, I felt being on social media is like asking for troubles. As soon as you get online you will be bombarded with same very question, Hey bro, have you got any job?, how much money you are making right now? They are your friends and actually, they enjoy your period of joblessness. Against your protection you have the only option to get offline as quickly as possible. Your presence on social media becomes rarity. And suddenly your friend will declare you as an extinct species like Dinosaur.

You will be the only one who can stand for you. You have to fight from extreme negative thoughts like attempting suicide. Will have to find a way out of depression because, no one will stand your sentiments, what's going through your mind. Even your family members will not give a shit for all these. They just think you are lazy and not trying enough. To make clear how having different attitude and psychology help, the story of Loki Alexendra being jotted down.

I am Loki Alexendra, currently working as a full time software engineer. I am a graduate pass out from Bilkent University. After a few hiccups in initial phase of my job search, I got one. And it was quite satisfying. Not that great but yes, enough to cheer about. More often than not when I used to be alone the same set of questions iterated throughout my mind i.e. Is this the job I was looking for? And is this the life I dreamt of? One simple answer of all such questions was a big No. I always loved to write a piece of code, programming and creating applications (Software). Because, right from my childhood I loved the computer games, fixing software related computer issues. I was not that brilliant but, I used to learn those things by watching videos on YouTube, reading books after books that were surely out of my syllabus. But, I continued to do so because it all kept me excited. I wanted to do something different and what I actually loved. I had a job of a bank manager. The salary was quite attractive. My family was happy. The quest to live my own life and have a dream job triggered me to jump out of the well. A bold decision was to be taken and in support of it I quit my job.

This was a stupid decision in my family and friend point of view and they were right for some reasons. Now, having said that the decision had already been taken, I became a certified unemployed. For quite a few days I again faced all the humiliation, frustration and whatever a jobless person have to go through. But, I always backed my decision of quitting the job. In order to prove myself right and have my dream job, I began to utilize my free time. A new freedom was found that surely was refreshing. Being jobless was indeed like a blessing for me. Now, I had all the time for what I was meant to do. To be straight, I must mention that this new found freedom lent me the opportunity to publish source code and release my android application that I was procrastinating for so long. Further, I published a number of source codes and in the process I ended up with a programmer job for a reputed company, the job that I loved to do. Now, I am purely enjoying my life. And most importantly, my family is happy along with me. My life is more adventurous now.

The story of Loki suggests that don't get too much affected by what joblessness brings to the table. Use your new freedom to rise above. Your future after unemployment depends on your psychology during unemployment. Joblessness does affect our emotion and the actions but it's our mental strength that uplift us spirit and help fighting our grey times.

CHAPTER 2

The Psychological Studies

2

The Psychological Studies

Once, Kasl & Cobb conducted a study related to unemployment. The study was on physical and emotional reactions to unemployment focused on blood pressure changes. The study was methodologically sound. He found that blood pressure levels during anticipation of job loss and unemployment or probationary re-employment were clearly higher than during later stabilization on new jobs, men whose blood pressure remained high longer, had more severe unemployment were lower on Ego Resilience, reported longer-lasting subjective stress and failed to show much improvement in reported well-being; within the period of anticipation, there was a clear rise in blood pressure which was correlated with subjective ratings of felt stresses... Further, as it progressed they found that since the two controlled groups don't showed significant changes in blood pressure. Anxiety, disorganization, depression, shame, humiliation, degradation, loss of self worth and confidence were noticed as the emotional outcomes of unemployment whereas these emotional reactions lead to increased consumption of alcohol, wife & child abuse, crime and suicide. These actions were marked as the physical reaction due to unemployment.

Responses to job loss vary depending on the psychology of the people. Researchers from Australia presented the fact that people who has high self-esteem and perceived control over their lives, and low for neuroticism, are best equipped to deal with unemployment.

In another psychological study in 2010 *Journal of Organizational Behavior*, Vol. 31, No. 5 revealed that men are more likely to see it as defeat while women take it as opportunity. For job loss survival perspective as per *Journal of*

Neuroscience, Psychology and Economics, Vol. 3, No. 32 researcher at the New York University School of Medicine and Columbia University in New York City found that 69 percent of 774 participants who lost their job reported a dip in life satisfaction at the time of job loss, but were back to their normal feel-good attitude a year later.

In spite of the fact that joblessness absolutely can be an open door, Goodman says, it's critical not to happily urge enduring customers to transform lemons into lemonade.

Sinking into joblessness can hinder the pursuit of employment, points out Peter Warr, PhD, a teacher emeritus at the Institute of Work Psychology at the University of Sheffield in England. "It's a terrible dilemma," he says. "If you don't feel bad, you don't want to get back to work." Warr is the author of "Work, Happiness, and Unhappiness" (Erlbaum/Routledge, 2007).

Amid the 1980s, Warr considered Sheffield steelworkers who lost their employments as the business crashed. Some moved toward becoming surrendered to their destiny, and essentially sat tight for the activity market to pivot. Others handled the issue usefully, discovering humanitarian effort or side interests to involve their opportunity. The last gathering was unquestionably more joyful — yet they were not hurrying to rejoin the work force (Journal of Social Issues, Vol. 44). The authors of a later 2007 survey likewise contend that dynamic jobless individuals are more joyful than their inert partners (Work: Journal of Prevention, Assessment & Rehabilitation, Vol. 28, No. 4).

In this way, psychologists must institute a sensitive adjustment: helping individuals build up the skill to make due without work, even as they keep on seeking work.

CHAPTER 3

Outcomes Of Joblessness

3

Outcomes Of Joblessness

As Joblessness sustaining for a considerable period brings a lot of changes to the human psychology and their action, it's very unlikely that the impacts will be positives. Most commonly negative outcomes are expected out of the negatives. So is the case of joblessness. A discussion on various byproducts of joblessness is to be discussed now.

Freedom

Being jobless what we achieve is a new found freedom that provides us the sense of exploring horizons, looking beyond the hidden opportunities. It looks very refreshing.

Imagine suddenly a day struck you hard; you lost your job that you loved. World goes upside down in first appearance. But, on the other hand when you give solace to your inner conscience, pat yourself, recollect your spirits and stand up for one more shot. After a few days of Stress, You will be enjoying your life. As you have not to follow the schedule that you were used to, you have no deadline to finish a task, no reasons to get up as early as possible and get dressed to go on duty. This new found freedom is actually a source of inspiration to create something new, mastering you, Knowing new skills and the opportunity to act on whatever positive ideas comes to your mind.

Frugality

Introduction of frugality to your lifestyle is one of the most prominent effects of being jobless.

What we do when we have no money or less than what actually required? Most obviously, the very first step we take is to cut short our expenditure. We tend to become too much selective of our choices of expenses. Our focus shift to start prioritizing our expense choices and act accordingly.

Since you are jobless you have no money to fulfill your own wish, forget the wishes of your family. Unless you have banked lots of money, it's hard to think of buying a car, to travel out with family. Since in today's world our relationships directly attached with our bank balance, we need to have a good job to hold up our relationships and friends. Maintaining relationship is difficult without money. Sometimes situation becomes so worse that even our basic requirement looks redundant to expense. In such case frugality is at peak.

Insecurity

Inception of the sense of insecurity is the worst of all the negatives that mushroomed out of the state of joblessness. How a jobless people treated by family, friends and society leads to the insecurity and lower self-esteem.

Your family and friend hammer you by the same advice for plenty of times like- be more confident, apply broadly, create network etc. And what you are getting only is rejection. Hearing these things consistently will eat up your self-esteem. As a result of it you will be losing your confidence more and more. Every time you will go for job interview, you will be less confident in comparison to the previous attempt. If this continued to persist for long, your confidence graph will hit the rock bottom. Besides this, the more you lose your self esteem and confidence more you will start questioning your worth. You will not feel you're relevant to the society. Quite interestingly your society will treat you the same as if your presence doesn't make any difference. Infusion of insecurity blocks your free flowing ideas through your mind. It will make you mentally too weak to even stand up for yourself. For example- Consider yourself sitting in a group having discussion on any topic. Since you have lost your confidence you will look reluctant to put forth your opinion. Even if you have immense belief in your ideas you will be afraid to share. Worst of all, you will cocoon up to counter your humiliation.

Annoyance

Habit of fretting out at even a small mistake becomes a common characteristic that branched out of joblessness. You will react more rudely than what actually required to show your disagreement on something. You will be grumpy if someone asks your future plan, getting advice from anyone without consulting them and so on. Annoyance will disturb the tranquility of your mind.

This will surely hamper your thoughts and your decision because a perturbed mind can't bring fresh ideas and complete sense of calmness. It's quite apparent that annoyance will come into existence when you spend a lot of money for your education, you study your butt off, and you continually sacrifice your health & family time. As a result of it you have no job to cheer upon. So, try to dowse down your anger in order to bring something new and inspirational.

Desperation

You can understand what desperation means specially in the case of finding a dream job. Desperation means you are fully pumped up from inside and anxious, all set to pounce upon opportunities, having willingness to push your limit to achieve something; still you are failing at this.

I found an unemployed once said; 'I apply to jobs I didn't want. I stopped thinking about the dream job I wanted. I just wanted any job. I don't even mind retail. I compromised. Application after application. The definition of insanity is repeating something over and over again expecting different results unless it applies to job hunting. I feel like I am definitely capable of proving myself in anything, but so far I haven't been given a chance.' Whatever he said depicts the level of frustration and desperation when you are not getting a job even if holding whatever it requires.

Resentment

Being typical human being that belongs to our society, it's quite apparent that to be envious of someone's success & happiness is a common thing to happen. You along with your family member show resentment, if get to hear that someone known got placed in an MNC or snatched up a government job.

We can digest the fact that people who were actually very talented got amazing job offers but, we can't digest if same thing happen in reverse case. The resentment gets added up if you came across the fact that someone got the job even if he didn't study as much, never went a school, and didn't have competitive edge. In that case the only question haunts us are, what did they do to get that job?

Humiliation

Humiliation is a state of mind based on experiences of rejection and loss of human dignity and self worth. I have got a sense of belief that people do judge one's value by knowing whether you are employed or not if you have the degree.

As an example I am engraving here my case. I received humiliation whenever anyone used to ask my parent regarding my unemployment status. I have not much friends. Only a couple to count, Abhishek Kumar and Tanmay Kishor. Perhaps the only positive for me is at least they never tried to poke me. They are cooperative. I have distanced myself more than a bit from social media because I dreaded the question, "What are you up to?" my bounce rate on social media got skied up. I feel humiliated every time my father remind me that they took bank loan for a flat only because he expected me to get a job and pay for it after my graduation. The thing didn't pan out how he anticipated. After my graduation I was in no mood to search a job that's why applied for regular master degree course that I recently completed.

At times, you also get humiliated by the fact that your family sacrificed so much time and money supporting you, and you feel like you've let them down. It actually sucks not being able to be very generous with my friends and family.

The humiliation of being jobless kills you every day.

Uncertainty

I don't know who suggested my father; he forced me several times to apply for a lecturer job outside India if the situation is murky in India. Specially, Canada. He used to suggest apply outside country, go travel. I never understand from where he collected that much confidence that foreign countries have a job protected in my name. I tell myself every now and then that I will have a good future but, I don't know how it will happen or when it will be.

PART 3

Congratulation! You Are Jobless

"We believe that if men have the talent to invent new machines that put men out of work, they have the talent to put those men back to work."

-John F. Kennedy

Congratulation!
You Are Jobless

My eyes are a little more lighted up as I begin to jot down this particular part of the book. I'm all pumped up for this. But firstly I ask you one thing, have you ever congratulated and patted yourself specifically for something that doesn't go down well with others? I guess, not so.

I ask you to please before doing something else stand in front of a mirror. Have a good look at yourself and then give a gentle pat on your back. Then looking back at yourself into the mirror utter ***"Congratulation you are jobless."*** Just do it first without asking any question. How you feel now as you do this? Perhaps more relaxed and calmed. Now, you can continue reading and enjoy the answers of all your queries.

Why This Congratulation?

I think you deserve a heartiest congratulation because of what you gain as a jobless. What you get are not at disposal even for a job protected people. You need to accept that "Time is happiness". Today we don't have time to spend on real source of happiness. Ask these questions to any of your employed friend, relatives or colleagues

Can you remember when the last time you talked to any of your best friend heart to heart?

Can you recall the time when you last went somewhere for a family holiday?

Or, can you just remember when you last laughed your heart out?

To recall all these will be very thorny to them because it's been so long and dried out of their memories. These things are not happening more often with most of the employed. Every people are in the mad race to reach somewhere. I don't understand why they are in such hurry, I guess, only to wait longer by reaching quickly.

This congratulation is for that precious gift which you have, The extra time. People who already having a job wish to have that extra time gifted because, while at job they are missing too many things that will make life wonderful.

On a lighter note the unemployed you, have plenty to cheer about:

- ℵ You are not supposed to rush everyday for a 9 to 5 job.
- ℵ You can spend all day at your favorite place with your family or friends if you desire.
- ℵ You got the freedom to spend quality time with your loved ones be it your girlfriend your wife or your children and not miss out a party.

- ℵ Freedom from daily rush forcing to hold your sit in traffic while back home.
- ℵ Freedom to go where you want.
- ℵ Freedom to follow your own schedule.
- ℵ Freedom and space for growing your own business.

So, basically in short I am congratulating you for the reason that you are about to get out of the rat race and begin to live life on your terms.

Job Security is the New Insecurity

Just for a piece of information the fact mentioned here what International Labour Organisation (ILO) has to say, only a quarter of total employed have job security. The rest of the three quarters are engaged in part-time jobs, contract based or in unpaid family jobs and any of these doesn't ensure the security. After finishing graduate degree it's heard that as soon as you get a job you have ensured security to your happiness, family well being and the survival.

What I found and noticed is a job security is the new insecurity. Almost, every working professional are living with constant fear of getting fired. I found my college professors securing a job but always living with insecurity to lose their job, I found the same with working professionals in private firm. They never know when will be their last day at that particular job. Believe me, a person having a job feel more insecure than who actually never got employed.

However, I am not only talking about this kind of security. It's of a new kind. The way you work like a robot just to clear your bills is only keeping you physically alive but not by soul. Because most of today's employed work force are underemployed. They have bargained with their terms of living.

Barring a little financial protection, a job in present scenario offers three major kind of insecurity:

א Health Insecurity
א Relationships Insecurity
א Life Insecurity

Health Insecurity: The average working hour for most of the employed is 9 to 5. Their leisure time gets smoked up in working and thinking about their boss. For that underpaid job people put their health at stake. The wild schedule has destroyed their lifestyle. They don't have leisure time to even look after their own body. They are deprived of sound sleep and to list out what should be taken in breakfast, lunch, dinner or refreshment. Eating burger, pizza or noodles will never ensure a good health. Your rough lifestyle can cost you the job.

Relationships Insecurity: You might have seen relationships falling apart, be it husband-wife relation, be it father-child relation or be it years old friendship. Who is to be blamed? It's the job people doing is the real culprit. The underpaid job bereaved you from spending quality time with your loved ones, friends and family. How someone can even think of spending quality time when he is sucked up working whole day that too without any real motivation, that's too much to ask for.

Especially when there is private job nothing is in your control, life is unbalanced. You have to give up control to get in control. Your grown up children will never understand your sacrifice because when the time was to enjoy their childhood you were managing financial problems and working hard to secure the family's future. Working for someone else for half of your life can secure family not the relation.

Life Insecurity: Can you imagine overwork causing death? Don't stress yourself thinking, it's happening. Japanese have termed the sudden death due to overwork as *Karoshi.* Reports clarify that about 10% sudden death of male is the result of overwork. Victimized families are successfully suing companies for partnering in sudden death of loved ones. Since we have compromised with our future unknowingly or knowingly we can't avoid these things to happen. Why? – Because securing a job made us more insecure. We presume thinking for health, family & relationships will bring down financial crisis at the drop of a hat. That's why in the quest of present, future is mostly insecure.

Your Life is Hell in a Cell

Are you a fan of WWE (World Wrestling Entertainment)? And especially of a match called Hell in a cell? Hang on for a minute. Just to let you know I must mention that I am not promoting WWE or the event. It's just a funny reference.

Even if you have never seen such match I request you to watch any one of the best hell in a cell match and then ask yourself; how was the experience? Have you enjoyed? Actually it doesn't matter you enjoyed it or not. I only asked you for the purpose to get the feel of the whole set up and the event. What I am saying is, you are experiencing or will be experiencing the same with your job. Your workplace is like the same whole setup of the match. Your opponent is your boss, your manager, your colleagues, the working environment or the combination of all. Why am I making this so repulsive statement? Because of the following prominent reasons that will make you believe that your job is nothing but a hell in a cell.

ℵ You are locked dawn whole day in the office clinging to your sit and chained to a desk. Is this the natural activity of a human being? No, it's purely unnatural.

ℵ As whole world falling a victim of economic slowdown you are supposed to get an excessive workload because of the business downsizing. For example – when I took admission in master degree the number of faculties were more than satisfactory. But, by the beginning of final semester it reduced to just 4 or 5 (Talking of an individual branch). As a result I have seen a single faculty handling almost every work.

ℵ You must not think of your position to be upgraded at least for 10 to 15 years because of your seniors who seems to have taken pledge to not to move anywhere. Because they are feared of moving somewhere else and getting a chance.

ℵ You have to share your work space with incompetents who are quite irritating and they only deserved to get fired long before.

- אּ You have go through the test of backstabbing, putting on fake smile and the cut throat competition.
- אּ No such freedom to put forth your ideas and views.
- אּ You will be subjected to be intermeddled constantly that will disrupt your productivity.
- אּ You must not expect cooperation from any departments. They are only to show their power. Teamwork is left only to be a compulsion.
- אּ You have to beg for vacation irrespective of the cause of taking leave, still quite unsure to get it.
- אּ The person supervising you will take credit of your work and ideas to be a hero in the eyes of the boss.
- אּ Your working hour is independent of your ability to produce effective result way ahead of schedule in comparison to the jerks.
- אּ You will be constantly surrounded by cage of bureaucracy, nonsense rules and the unmotivated dead faces.
- אּ To hold your position or job you have to be yes-man of your seniors.

- ℵ No such real appreciation, acknowledgement and recognition for being exceptional in your work.
- ℵ And the worst of all what you will get in return to all these is a salary that will somehow clear your bills and for savings you will have to dump various requirements or plans.

What you think of your workplace after all this? Will you still be enjoying being in hell? If yes, it means you are completely unaware and unknown to yourself.

Why to produce just a piece if it can be a masterpiece?

You loving your job and quite satisfied with what you are doing right now, it's great not everyone are that lucky. And I too don't want to divert or confuse you. But, if not then you are making hell out of everything. Right now by working for others what are you doing is selling your services or creating products for other to sell them. Since you are not motivated enough either mentally or financially you are creating just a piece. Probably, a piece of shit. When every other people creating the same piece what could you expect, an increment in position and salary, a certification of individual brilliance or words of appreciation? It's all foolish to ask, I reckon.

If you don't get a wakeup call until now, you will be creating the same piece for your entire life. You must think of creating a masterpiece instead of just a piece because you are capable of.

What's called a masterpiece?

From personal perspective just to make it short and clear a masterpiece can be perceived as anything flawless and unique. It could be a piece of art, a book, a speech, a business, an idea, a goal or any other thing.

A corporate or underpaid job kills your creativity, skill and downshift your personal intelligence. Creation of a magnum opus doesn't happen overnight. It requires perseverance, devotion, descipline and the most important patience along with a bit of personal intelligence. If you can gel all this properply, you are just an inch away from creating a magnum opus. Your real success in life will not be determined by your bank balance or your professional position but by knowing the art to depict a masterwork. Your one masterpiece idea can transform your fate provided the idea must be responded with an action.

To be a picasso or shakespeare you must devote yourself like not every people can. To create a masterpiece you have to be on the top of your game. The picasso whom the world know today have just a few masterpiece in the name out of 100,000 plus artworks. What driven them to pinnacle is the hard work, perseverance and belief. Missing any one of these will never produce the result. Basically, creating a masterpiece is the process of trial and error. It is more about producing more and more untill you have one.

Becoming A Millionaire

You can be a millionaire only by becoming your own boss, it will never happen working for others. If I am wrong then please kindly suggest me just one example of becoming a millionaire by doing a job for someone else. Believe me it never happened and never will even if you sacrifice your entire life by doing so.

So very first thing I like to ask, are you ready to live life on your own terms? Are you ready to be a millionaire? I am quite sure your reply will be in yes. Now, what next? – A solid great business idea. But, more than a business idea it requires one thing called 'belief'.

Belief Vs Illusion

Having belief into something is great but, a hollow belief is nothing but an illusion. For example – Believing yourself of starting your own company is your belief but thinking of generating loads of money without challenges is your illusion. Also, believing your product will be the game changer is your belief but it will be accepted by everyone because you think of it a masterpiece is your illusion. Basically, what I percieve about belief is if your thought is too harsh to the associated outcome irrespective of the situations then it becomes an illusion. Belief is something that keep your eyes open while illusion is something that brings a virtual curtain in front of your vision.

If you are missing self belief you can create it. Because, every belief of human beings has developed on three things:

ℵ What you experience?

For example – If we have had witnessed a miracle our belief on god's existence got stronger. Further, my experience about writing the first book "The Art of Great Research Writing" made me believe I can and getting sold made my belief rock solid that empowered me to continue writing.

ℵ What others have to say about you?

It's something I call your outer programming. For example – When my sister and friend consistently told me I have enough ability and knowledge to write a book, it begin to lay a foundation of belief. Likewise when anyone make you believe what you can do your best and you do is creating belief in you.

✶ And, what's your perception about yourself?

This I call as programming the inner-self. This will be fruitful while holding your spirits and beliefs when you are up against odd. Always have a positive attitude about yourself. Simply think, you are unique, you are here for a purpose and act accordingly.

Starting your own business

Now, you got the very first element 'The belief'. What needed next is a great business idea. An idea driven by someone else can't set up a successful business or just copying others will not deliver the goods. Your ideas and business plan should be fresh and executable. So, where does a great idea will come from? It's definitely not about thinking of producing new Microsoft, Google or Facebook. Its also not about becoming another Jeff Bezos or another Donald Trump. It's more about a new and unique you who can have answers to the questions like "How can I improve on this?" or "Can I do this better or differently from the other guy doing it over there?" Or simply, "Is there market share not being served that makes room for another business in this category?"

The best ways to find a great business idea

ℵ What perturbs you?

A thing that disturbs you is nothing but a business opportunity. Colin Barceloux was very perturbed by the fact that college textbooks were too costly to buy. This very thought irked him and in 2007, two years after graduating, he decided to take action and founded Bookrenter.com, a San Mateo, Calif.-based business that offers textbook rentals at about a 60 percent discount. What began as a one-man operation created out of frustration now has 1.5 million users and 200 employees. "You just have to look at what frustrates you," he says. "There's your business idea right there."

ℵ What's next? – Trends & Scopes

Follow and act according to the trends is another business idea. Successful business ideas are about trends and technologies on the horizon and how you might move into those areas, says Sergio Monsalve, partner at Norwest Venture Partners, a Palo Alto, Calif.-based venture capital group. He suggests, for example, thinking about innovations related to the living room and home entertainment systems now that companies like Apple are developing new television technologies. "What can that mean in terms of new ways to live in your house and be entertained?" he says.

✄ Play with price

Playing with price is the most common game various startup companies kick start their business by. Just play with the price of existing products. Take Warby Parker, an eyeglasses company launched in 2010 by four business school friends. The New York-based business sells prescription glasses, which are typically priced at $300 or more, for $95. Since its launch, it has grown to 100 employees.

ℵ Check your skills related entirely new possibility

Think about your skills and whether they might be useful in a new area, suggests Bill Fischer, professor of innovation management ?at IMD?, the top-rated Swiss business school, and co-author of *The Idea Hunter: How to Find the Best Ideas and Make them Happen* (Jossey-Bass, 2011). Consider, for example, JMC Soundboard, a Switzerland-based company that builds high-end loudspeakers. Jeanmichel Capt invented the speaker by applying his experience building guitars as a luthier, using the same resonance spruce to create a loudspeaker that produces a high-quality sound and looks like a sleek wood panel. There's also Providence, R.I.-based Dear Kate, a company founded by Julie Sygiel, who used her training in chemical engineering to create a stain-resistant, leak-proof underwear material that active women can use without worrying about menstrual leakage during a workout.

ℵ Do the new to the new

What new pop up in the market? Exercise Your eyeballs by looking for a room for business into it. Don't reinvent, redesign it. Take a look at what some of the big players in an industry are missing and figure out if you can fill the gaps, Key says. In 2003, for instance, he started the company Hot Picks, now based in San Jose, Calif., after realizing the major brands in the guitar pick industry weren't offering collectible novelty picks. Key designed a skull-shaped pick that filled an empty niche and was sold in 1,000 stores, including Wal-Mart and 7-Eleven. "The big guys leave a tremendous amount of opportunity on the table," he says.

ℵ Play the game – Mix & Match

Walk up and down the aisles of a drug, hardware or toy store combining two products across the aisle from each other into one, Key says. That should spark quite a few ideas, but be prepared for most of them to be bad. "You will come up with all these horrible ideas, and every once in a while you will find some brilliant idea out there," he says.

✂ Meet the needy

To come up with an idea that meets people's needs, there's no better way than by talking to shoppers and the needy one. If you are interested in sports bikes, hang out in the aisles of sports and bike shops and ask customers what they wish they could find in the marketplace. If you're interested in developing an e-commerce business, consider sending an online survey to potential customers to learn about their needs and interests.

Before you start any business, ask yourself these questions first:

What am I most passionate about?

What do I know about?

What do people ask me advice about?

What am I really good at doing?

What do I have experience doing?

What do I think about all the time?

What do I love talking about?

Answers of all these question will show you the clear picture, what business idea will be the best suited to you. Disclaimer here is be loyal to yourself while answering all these question.

Why everyother will never have their own business?

Do you wonder why every people don't do certain things even if they think that will be great to do? Let's take a simple example of 'Yoga'. We all know performing yoga will only benefit & bring your body in great shape. Still very few people practice it. Is this the lack of time which is to be blamed? No. I've seen many people expensing their time over stupid things and sleeping whole day. In fact you should never have time issue because successful people have more work than you and believe me they still find a place in their schedule for yoga or excercises, not necessarily for a lenghty exercise, it could be gentle stretch, few push-ups or little bit of jogging.

So why its not happening? The best answer is our nature & attitude. Firstly, human nature is always reluctant for a change. We don't accept any changes very easily. Your encounter with various problems are destined to happen as soon as you start rolling your dice. And most probably most of you will be done and dusted then and there even without tasting any sort of success. The best way to handle your problems are:

a) Always expect the unexpected. Program yourself in such a way that a problem should appear as normal encounter.
b) Create a sense of gratitude towards your problems. Think the otherway that you are so responsible that god has chosen you to accomplish that particular job. And no other person can do that better than you.

Other reasons why most of you will not even think of doing your own business are:

➢ Your lethargic attitude.
➢ Nature of procrastination.
➢ Lack of courage to take risk
➢ Lack of Self control & discipline
➢ Lack of belief & determination
➢ You are not passionate enough
➢ Fear of failure

Zero in on passion, desire & determination

To hit right in bull's eye just get zero in on these three things – passion, desire & determination.

Passion: For starting your business if you don't want to do the research before selecting an area, its fine. But, do one thing - get into yourself and focus on your passion. Your passion will be the source of inspiration and motivation to propell you with one such successful idea. The biggest advantage of following your passion is it will keep you pumped up especially in the beginning when you have to spend more hours on your business than what you actually like. That extra work will be like an adventure when you choose a business for which you are passionate about. What you like or dislike will give you an hint to know your passion. But, its not always possible to know exactly all likes and dislikes about certain business. In most of the cases the key is to get started with whatever ideas comes to you. Because, waiting and looking for a better idea to respond will never happen. There will never be a perfect time either to start your business. Kick start from where you are.

You will fail in your first couple of attempt but, most importantly you will get experience. Every initial business venture will be a new learning curve for you. Relying on your passion will also help you to stay happy and motivated independent of the business outcomes. After all ultimate aim of our life is to spend a happy life. A person can earn millions but if not passionate about his work then he will not be happy and throw it all the away under pressure.

If you are driving your business with passion then:

- ♣ Your life will be properous, meaningful and well directed.
- ♣ You will have the strength to fight attrocities and handle failures.
- ♣ Your life will be full of adventures.

Desire & Determination: The 2Ds will drive toward success through every barrier. After passion you got to have a very strong desire that's called *a burning desire.* This burning desire will force you to dream big. And a big dream will unrest you to take action. Since, you will not have entrepreneur skill, your encounter with numerous challenges will force you to give up. In that case *a pig-headed determination* will be the saving grace for you. Your determined vision will help you to overtake any problems. You will be ready 24x7 to pay the price for what it will take to be successful.

Create a leader in you

Although I'm not going to pen down a huge section on leadership skills but, will be discussing some of the best laws of leadership in brief. You getting started with own business means you are already on the way to lead others who will be working under you. To carry whole business on your own shoulder will need you the leadership qualities. What leaders do to handle different phases of their business? Although some of the things discussed earlier like, belief, passion, desire & determination are the character traits of a leader but, besides these there are certain other laws of leadership that must not be overlooked:

♣ A leader must be a big dreamer. Your dream will transfer in your follower that will propell them to work.

- A leader must be able to influence others. You must know how to communicate with different people and convince them to believe in your action & business module.

- A Leader must have a positive attitude in all case scenario. Should expect a positive result but must be able to handle success as well as failure.

- The Leader always lead by an example. You see what's the difference between a manager & a leader? A manager just convey how to do it and then sit relaxed & observe but, a leader tells how to do it & sets an example.

- The Leader is a strong decision maker.You must be able to take decisions if needed at the drop of a hat. You can't always rely on others to make a decision. But, also not to ignore them completely while taking any decision.

- The Leader has the highest levels of integrity and character.

- The Leader always exhibits persistence and determination to sail the ship to the destination.

Who made it big when down and out: The jobless stories

Here are some of the success stories which are personally close to my heart that will certainly inspire others as well. These real stories will also make you believe that you can do wonderful things being jobless.

As there are lots of success stories of jobless are available all over the place, I'm not putting here random examples rather a more profound, systematic & well researched. Every real success stories pens a different character & methodologies of jobless to overcome the unemployment.

Opportunity right in the backyard

I was quite mesmerized when I first came across this through an online community newspaper 'The Daily Dot'.

Joe Raineri lost his job working in construction when economy sinked way back in 2008. His wife had also no work either to feed six children. They both had got their age. His wife Lisa took initiative and decided to make some money for survival.

But, where was that opportunity hiding? – right in their backyard. Lisa piled up the wooden pieces lying in their backyard and in no time she created a beautiful designer table with Joe's support. Next they looked for option to get sold and soon came across craiglist- a classified advertisement website. As soon as they listed their product 50 people showed their willingness to buy and soon it was sold for $600.

This little success inspired them to produce more such masterpieces which eventually propelled Joe & Lisa Raineri to establish their own full time furniture business in 2010. And this way Terra Amico was born which latter went on to produce several other wooden furniture like Dressers, Bed frames, Headboards, Barn Doors, Wall Cladding, Chair & Stools, Light Fixtures, Fireplace Mantles, Dining Tables, Console Tables, Coffee Tables, Kitchen Islands, Kitchen Cabinets, Bars & Back Bars, Candle Holders, Planter Boxes. Now they not only produce furnitures they also deliever class on wooden artistry to others.

From nowhere to everywhere

Can you believe of becoming a billionaire only by writing books? Well, its happening and had happened already. This is the story of the first female billionaire author. Most of you have already gussed it, i think so. If not then just continue reading.

It all started with an idea and passion towards writing but only to be hindred continuously by tear-jerking miseries. She first got knocked down by the devastating death of her mother. At least for that time the idea of writing got ceased. To hold herself she moved to Portugal and got a job of an english teacher. There she decided to use her leisure time to continue writing the book. The completion of the book was planned by the time she returns from Portugal but only to be remained as a plan.

She got her second major setback when she witnessed her failed marriage. She lost her job. And, left alone to feed two mouths along with a baby daughter. When she found she had nothing to lose and it can't get worse than this she resumed her writing working in cafes while daughter fall asleep.

She tried her fate by sending manuscript of first three chapters but only to get rejected. This was followed by numerous rejections before finding her first publisher to read at Bloomsbury Publishing company. But more than the publisher it was editor's 8 years old daughter who showed her willingness to read more of it that forced the publisher to accept the manuscript. She left with a warning as well from publisher to get a job as writing children's books will not help her cause.

But, forget all these rest is history. The success of that first book "*Harry Potter*" followed with the success of "*Sorcerer's Stone*" which produced the JK Rowling the world know today. The Harry Potter series collected over $400 million in book sales. Through adaptation of her works into movies and sponsorship she went on to become first female billionaire author from being jobless. Her driving force was her passion for writing, her perseverance and belief to get success. All these things helped her to overcome numerous failures and rejections.

The story of inko's white tea

Even a small things can be a big thing if you are curious and passionate enough. The story of inko's white tea is one such example.

Andy Schamisso used to work in public relation but he was drained out and hated his job the most. But, somehow in the quest of survival he was stretching out himself to hang in. One day his wife asked him to find the rare available white tea that she used to take it everyday.

Andy began to hunt white tea over internet and during this course he came to know the health benefits of the white tea. By the way if you don't know white tea is the rare kind of tea which is helpful in reducing risk of cancer, cardiovascular disorder, and improvement in oral health It has antioxidant and anti-aging properties which help in maintaining good health and wrinkle free skin. It protects skin from the harmful effects of UV light. With its antibacterial properties, white tea protects the body from various infection causing bacteria.

As soon as Schamisso embraced all the interesting facts he soon got inspired to transform this into a big opportunity and a permanent source of income. He soon decided to make the white tea's recipe of his wife to other as well. So, he decided to call it quit his 13 years long career in public relation. Initially, Andy raised required funds and produced 6000 samples of the Inko's white tea which was named after his dog. To milk his hard work he roamed the street of New York. Soon he found his feet in market by reaching out to all the dedicated shops of white tea. This turned out to be a big success which kicked his income through selling out truckloads. Latter Andy established this business by transforming this into a company. Although, white tea were already available in the market but, Andy Schamisso decided to present it differently and more refreshing than others. He launched 14 different flavored varieties of Inko's white tea. What make his product unique from others are qualities like low in sugar, Fewer calories- Inko's bottle contains 50 calories....just enough to make it taste perfect!, refreshing flavors, organic etc. To know more why his product stand out visit inkotea.com. Had he just bought another white tea for her wife and overlooked this opportunity you hadn't been reading this story. So, keep your eyes open all the time you will find such career transforming business idea that will actually define your identity.

Boss - Lay Me Off

This is the story of Jim Wood, Founder & CEO of MateVeza — the first mate-infused beer of its kind in the world.

Jim used to work as commercial real estate analyst at Deutsche Bank for 5 years. In November 2008, a round of lay off started in the company. This likely could have been a major setback for Jim like all others but, the layoffs at his company turned out to be a blessing in disguise. "I knew my full support was critical for MateVeza's success," he told MainStreet. "The severance and unemployment being offered by Deutsche Bank was the perfect opportunity to jump into a business which was just an outcome of a hobby.

It all started with Berkeley's Oak Barrel legend Homer Smith's advice to a thirteen sixteen year old school boy having summer off from school. He started home brewing after seeing an ad for Berkeley's Oak Barrel wine craft. He planned it very simple: just boil the beer and transfer it into a fermenter before parents get back to home. Soon reality struck when one day jim's mom return home earlier than usual. As per Jim – The wrong timing of it to happen as he was adding hops to a dangerously full kettle, and witnessed an epic boil-over. The pungent aroma of hops flooded the neighborhood; beer flooded the garage. Surprisingly, Jim's mom looked supportive to his son. She not only helped clean up, but also promised not to convey Jim's dad.

Jim's brewing career was off to a good start, until storm of jim's dad hit the jim's deck. This time, everything looked catastrophically opposite of the previous encounter with mom. Jim's dad discovered the bubbling brew, and was in no mood to spare his son. But, quickly Jim's mind struck an idea to make dad a taste of his first American Ale just before dad grabbed a baseball bat, and threatened to smash the carboy — and young Jim's brewing dreams. Soon after getting taste of it dad let his son continue, for a hefty paternal excise tax: a sample of every beer he made.

For Jim, a taste of that first batch of beer was just as revelatory. With one sip, a passion blossomed, and soon after, so did a business. In 2003, by now an experienced homebrewer, Jim decided to experiment with marrying the flavors of his favorite California

IPAs with the natural buzz of yerba mate, a South American tea he drank to fuel his late-night brewing, studying — sessions. That union became MateVeza — the first mate-infused beer of its kind in the world — and its commercial success enabled Jim and his good friend and partner, Matt Coelho, to open Woods Beer's original brewpub, a small cafe on the corner of San Francisco's Dolores Park, in 2012.

So, coming back to the point when layoff started by the time Jim had already launched his organic bear – MateVeza which he was promoting doing night duties and weekends whenever not working 9 to 5. Now, Jim was not living in fear of being laid off as he got an option of his own to run a company. That's why Jim himself realized and asked his boss politely to please lay me off. They had a lot of success when they've been able to give customers samples and tell them their story. Today, MateVeza is joined by hundreds more adventurous brews, made and served at a growing network of pubs and brewing outposts, and Jim is happy to be at the helm. MateVeza is currently in California, Oregon, Washington, Nevada and Colorado and aiming to rule all over the globe.

A Jobless Became Multi-Entrepreneur

Specifically, this story must not be taken as some other example of successful jobless. It's not a story its whole of a journey.

Ten years prior to the age of 24, Michel Issa – A Swedish boy dreamed of becoming a monk. He had chosen this path with a passion & strong desire to make a difference for people. He sacrificed his almost 10 years of life for this purpose. But, only at the age of 24 he realized that by then his dream was no longer of becoming a monk as he felt that he could make a major difference outside of the monastery walls.

He then in 2011 decided to dump the idea of becoming a monk and returned his native place Sweden. Michel as a jobless started looking for a regular job for survival. But, he found himself terribly drowned out after applying for hundreds of jobs just to receive a NO every time. The last when he dreamed of a job was at McDonald before this too got shattered when McDonald's told him they had moved on with other applicants. After this rejection Michel's self-esteem & confidence hit the bottom rock.

These setbacks pushed Michel Issa to feel alienated. He had a positive attitude that lifted his spirit to think of this alienation towards entrepreneurship. He started a company acquiring cheap conference facility in Östergötland that nobody wanted followed by a Christian camp that no one looked interested because of the heavy price. Then in quest of saving his failing company in debt he decided to raise funds from people outside of religious and non-profit organizations but again only to embrace failure. He apparently learnt that having no network at all is blocking his success. Michel began networking and then came a huge turning point in his fate. He got an opportunity by chance to get in touch with the organization Greenpeace that booked their annual meeting there. This exposure soon brought a lot of success to Issa as he began to find his calendar booked for his conference facility business.

With this success he realized the importance of associating with people and decided to extend his network. This idea was supported by the step to write an email to successful business owners, millionaires and entrepreneurs explaining his identity, vision, purpose & asking them if they can meet. Well, smart enough – he got his list of these people by googling. Sending friend request on facebook didn't helped much but LinkedIn did. Eventually, he got yes! from serial entrepreneur and investor Gunilla von Platen. The meeting was organised at her office at one of the most expensive streets in Stockholm, Strandvägen. As she asked what he wants, Michel's answer was very simple – *"I just want to get to know you."* After an hour of meeting they got a picture together that opened new doors of opportunity for Michel when he posted that picture with Gunilla on facebook. From then onwards he also smartly used that picture sending with email to every well known business leaders. Also, he became more proactive to follow every industry leaders in networking events and introduce himself. This way he met Sweden's richest and most powerful businesswoman Antonia Ax:son Johnson and other that driven him into powerful rooms in business. Today, as an international public speaker and owner of several successful companies he cites the importance of networking as *"By networking you build up your own character. You meet a lot of people and build valuable contacts that can be of help for you to reach your goals. And in addition to that you learn a lot from other people. It creates opportunities."*

Within three years after he was unemployed, he has received several major awards, among others, Entrepreneur of the Year 2014 that he received from the King of Sweden, Social entrepreneur of the year 2014, the future leader 2014, the super talent of the year 2013 etc.

For Michel entrepreneurship is about bringing people together to make a difference in people's lives. Through his fascinating journey & lectures he gives many practical tips from his own life experience on how to succeed as an entrepreneur.

PART 4

Learning The Lessons

"What is the good of being a genius if you cannot use it as an excuse for being unemployed?"

-Gerald Barzan

CHAPTER 1

What You Learnt From Joblessness?

What You Learnt From Joblessness?

Remember yourself committing any mistake in the past. I mean anything right from your childhood to the adulthood.

As I remember, once I touched a hot frying pan unknowingly. Perhaps 3 years of age then. I had never felt before anything that hot. I cried my heart out. My epidermis got reddish. My mom came running in, Hugged tightly. She tried blabbing to divert my mind so that I forget to cry on my injury. Credit goes to her, she succeeded in it. That incident taught me a lesson not to touch anything fiery with bare hand.

Like this small incident, there will be a lot of stories to ponder. And I am quite sure you had taken a lesson out of every incident. What I am trying to convey is every problems exists in this world come up with a lesson to learn. The problem of joblessness must also be seen through the same lens. The teachings that consist with unemployment could only be seen by a positive person. Most of the unemployed people don't learn anything because their thoughts get diluted. They get blinded. Our perception, perseverance and the virtue of an optimist help us to learn and fight the atrocities. As we will progress into this chapter, we will learn the various lessons.

The Game of patience

I have immense patience. And I proudly consider it as my strength. Do you consider your patience the same? If you have this by birth then it's great. But if not, most probably job search throughout the unemployment phase will teach you. You will master the art of being patient even through your toughest of times.

Moreover, you will embrace this sooner or later for your survival even if you successfully bag a job. Because, your boss will always be like a famished cat all set to pounce upon a helpless rat.

This is how your boss acts.

And this is how you react.

You can find and punish me for comparing you with a rat. I beg sorry for this. You are a born lion as you think of yourself. But I can't help it. See, if you can act as a lion in front of your dreaded boss? I don't think so. You are smart.

You won't like that boss having another opening for you i.e a door out. You will try to ensure job security at first. You will never want that your name making the list of the jobless.

Whatever the work you do, it demands a certain level of patience as far as accomplishment of the goal is concerned. Barring the job search, you do a lot of work that looks challenging. But, sometimes even if you give your best shot, the outcome doesn't justify your effort as everything is not in our control.

The whole job search process is tiring & frustrating. You have to run through the internet & weed out news papers in order to secure birth for a job interview. We all have a process to approach towards our goals. But, it doesn't come up with a guarantee that the process will work and when it will work. We can do our part only as best as possible. It also happens at times that certain action proves wrong for an individual but the same process appears fruitful to others. Like, when you were a college student, you had prepared for your exam following a certain sets of rules and strategies that had of your own. Sometimes you might have shared the same with your friend.

Both of you had followed it strictly but, it might have happened that your friend had ended up with better marks than you. Considering same questions were attempted with almost same short of contents value. In that case, you envy your friend's success.

I'm incorporating all these out of my experience. It happened to me during college days. I figured out, why? Our results may sometimes depend on our luck, sometimes on our personal way of representing something differently than others and sometimes our level of preparation.

It does suggest that everything can never be in our control. What we can do is to follow *"Hope for the best and prepare for the worst."* At the end of the day we have to be patient and can pray and wait for our turn to cheer up.

Throughout my job search process I never lost my patient. I think myself gifted with this. Yes, I went low occasionally after rejection but my patient level was rock solid.

Now, consider yourself snatching an opportunity of your bread and butter. If you work for a private firm, you have to perform out of your skin. Most of our friends had decided to end their academic education after engineering. And they are working in private multinational companies. They are loaded with words of wisdom and highly authoritative words of their senior. They seem irritated. Their reaction shows their frustration. They are impatient. But, they can't help it. They try to hold on themselves and being practical with what they learnt when they were jobless, i.e. the patient.

Let Go Attitude

We all are brought up on earth with a lot of expectations. Isn't it? Your parent had expected many out of you as you had opened your eyes the very first time. Humans are made up of countless expectations.

The very basic and common expectation behind bringing you into this beautiful world is the expectations of your parent that you will take guard of them in their old age.

We are taught to live up to someone's expectation that had belief in our ability. If you help someone, you expect something in return. There will always be someone expecting something from you. Coming to the case of getting a job, your entire dear one expects you getting a job as soon as your education drawn to a close.

Like being more patient, unemployment also teach us to let go of expectations. I had learnt this art. I was compelled to embrace let go attitude as I was getting earthed under the expectations. At times it becomes vastly difficult to let go of the expectations while you look reluctant to accept your defeat at the hand of your circumstances. You should constantly remind yourself that as long as you put your effort in, it will lead to an astonishing outcome. When you pass over expectations it will ease out your psychological pressure. You will feel free to express. You won't be subdued.

But, one thing to just remind you, it could be mistaken by you that letting go of expectation suggest to giving up. There is brightest of chance that most of you will consider both things as same.

I am your friend, perhaps better than many of your physical friends. I will guide you cautiously. That's why I decided to make everything clear to prevent you from misinterpreting something. Don't hollow out your own conclusion out of something that misleads you. Coming back, now we need to understand the difference between letting go and giving up.

Let go of Vs giving up

I reckon if you have got it right what let go attitude means. In a nut shell letting go of something suggest dumping that particular thing temporarily whereas giving up indicates that you put your last attempt to achieve your goal. After that you will never chase it.

Giving up, label you that you have succumbed to the adversity. You no longer want to get your dream job or simply you are no longer after getting a job.

Is giving up is a solution to your problems? – Certainly not. So, instead of collapsing under the burden of your expectations and giving up, chase your dream until you get. In the hindsight, try to create your own source of possibilities and opportunities.

It's not the end of the world

We are becoming too critical of ourselves when it comes to successful completion of any goal or a desire. Whether it's a job, a new home, a luxury car, having kids, having dinner at an expensive hotel or spending holiday in Alice's wonder land, the happiness of life lies even in getting there, not in the final jubilance.

When you were a kid, it had happened to you that you demanded something like getting your favorite ice-cream, toys, clothes or something else, and that had not been fulfilled. What you deed then? Did you decided to end your life for that? Surely, no. Also consider when you greatly expected something like getting top in your exams and failed at it. Did you think of committing suicide? Yes, there are people who think of suicide even after failing at smallest of things, but I am not talking about them. They are the born coward. So, why you not end life that easily for these things? Because you never given those things that importance. What you did being a smart student is to move forward and focus on next opportunity -Right? As it's not the end of the world. Life is filled with opportunities, we need to be alert to recognize and grab it.

"Life is not a bed of roses"

Moreover, do you ever think that whatever we desire is all achievable? - It can never be. You notice if everything in your life is easy, serene and peaceful, chances are very high that you aren't learning and growing. No matter how good or bad your time is, if life looks stagnant it means your personal growth has got a stumbling block. Being a potential job hunter, remember life will never be easy for you. Either prior to your job search process or the post job search. Everything going your way according to your plan, wish or desire means you are defying one of the most prevalent proverbs – *"Life is not a bed of roses"*. Also, if life is always been kind to you then you are the luckiest of the luckiest. My heartiest congratulation to you if this is the case. But, I know if it's been so then you are not supposed to hold this book and read patiently. (Joking ...)

Finding a job is a real can of worms. You have to go through a lot of ups and downs, atrocities and bitter experiences. You should embrace all these gracefully. Because, the thing we achieve fighting tooth and nail always look pleasant, heartening and heavenly. Whenever you feel low when you receive rejection and feel frustrated, do one thing – recall an incident from past when you achieved something through putting a lot of effort and your reaction post the achievement. It could be the smallest of things. Believe me it is our tendency to get happy for every bit of success. Recall how you became excited and cheerful when you first created your Gmail and face book account. Probably you had perceived it as getting through an interview or a competitive exam. When you act upon this you will derive a source of motivation and inspiration for future prospect.

The Future Preparation

One of the good things you learn when you search for job as a fresher is - how to get prepared for future?

I'm talking here about future preparation in the context of joblessness. If you have gone through the very first chapter "Through The Realities"; I guess, You have got an idea about how the world economy behaving and where our employment opportunities heading towards due to present nature of the economy. If you agree with me getting a job never guarantee that you will never become a jobless again. So what we do is cast our eyes down and focus on what we have at present. If we begin to look at future of our present job then we tend to become restless and much more insecure than ever before.

Statistically speaking, our economic slowdown forcing employers to go for the hiring on contractual or temporary basis. This suggests that most number of people having a job today is going to be jobless tomorrow. Because, there will be sometimes off between the jobs. Same will be the case if there will be switch off between jobs by choice. Consider another situation i.e. Layoff. Almost every prominent organization executes the process of layoff as a part of their structural revamp. Recently Multinational companies like L&T, Infosys and some ecommerce companies laid off thousands of employees as part of their revival of business strategies. When asked about getting laid off for multiple times some of the job searching people revealed that second time getting a job was easier than before as they were better prepared than before. Now, they have grown up with enhanced networking and job search skills.

Redesigning Yourself

When you get laid off or having a transition between jobs, you can chisel down your personality, polish your skill or to enlarge the list of your skills.

You can do anything that excite you and add value either personally or professionally. Besides, you can find new interest in something that could appear as hobby at first but who knows that it could become a permanent source of your income and possibly it may end up as turning into your own business. And then it would be the case that once you were searching for a job but, now you will be hiring others for your business. Always look to redesign and reincarnate yourself, try even if you are untroubled.

I've Love Affair, Do You...?

"You show immense love to whatever work you do and always look to reflect perfection in your work", Once quoted one of my master degree friend, Sandeep Sharma. This nice complement was for me. My face flashed up with a gentle smile. I am not used to such beautiful complements more often. Well, I never noticed this about myself before. But, at times the thought of a perfectionist does come to my mind. But, I defy it myself as for me there is no existence of thing like perfection. There is always a better way to do something.

I always put the labor of love at display. It gives me immense serenity. And this never meant to harness praise from random faces. To live a cheerful and productive life you must develop a love affair with your work. Consider a day, you wake up and realize that money is the only reason you dread to do certain work, think of it as a day to move on and find a new direction. If you think you are not enjoying your job, stop doing. Your time is more worth than that. Unemployment has taught many that filling heart is more important than filling bank balance.

You should be afraid and reluctant to put your foot into the world that consists of an irrelevant job, absence of love and lack of motivation. If not finding the job you would die up to do then probably consider your own creative endeavor. Feel fulfilled as a creator and gather wits and appreciation while meeting some great people along the way.

A love affair with something makes the whole journey a cake walk, memorable, joyful, cherishing and living. Probably you all should give a thumb up for this thought, for me, not necessarily but if agreed. I am strong believer of the fact that whatever attitude and virtue we try to incorporate is already suppressed somewhere beneath ourselves. If you're doubtful, remember your childhood and imagine the same current scenario putting in place yourself as innocence and innovative child rather than a grown beast by physique but not by psyche. Answers to all your queries will be right in front of you.

As I move further, I have instantly plucked an example right from my childhood. My father has always been very hard when it comes to education of children. He used to be very rude and strict while we (My elder sister, a younger brother and I) used to study. At the back of our mind, we always had a feeling to get punished heavily and un-judicially for almost everything and anything. There was a strict as well as hectic routine of study to follow every day. We had thought that probably, we were the only children on this planet without even a single holiday. After a very late night study we were forced to wake up study at 3:00 AM that continued to an hour prior to school time. But, as time progressed and I turned 13, got freed up by that boring routine.

Now, this was only for my other two siblings. I got license to have my own norms, rules and regulations freedom to implement. I started to study without being intervened by father. I began to show love for books through myself rather than being forced that always seemed a burden. A love affair between books and me started to groom. Whenever, I got a free time I chosen study over meaningless enjoyment. These all got noticed by my father and I was awarded a freedom to have my own schedule. I began to study more and enjoy it more than when I was commanded by father. I never felt bored and suppressive right after that freedom. My productivity got increased. And, knack to not get perturbed by difficulties infused in me while studying.

This is indeed a reality that if you love a work or job wholeheartedly, then you will never get too much perturbed by any difficulties and will have all the strength to fight back and get a solution. A work only look a burden and tedious when you don't love and enjoy it.

CHAPTER 2

I Offer You A Talisman

I Offer You A Talisman

Joshua a neighbor of mine, a frustrated graduate, once talking to me revealed that his parent was out of town and he was planning to paint the town red. I denied his proposal to ensure my participation as I'm a little bit more conservative. He never minded it though. As the conversation progressed I went on to ask, "Why your parent left you all alone?"

"They never wanted me to know exactly", Joshua replied. Everything was secret.

After a gap of two weeks we encroached at a coffee shop. Conversation was random. Suddenly, my eye got stuck on a little square shaped thing hanging around his neck, supported with a black thread.

I asked, "What's that thing around your neck?"

It's called a Talisman, he replied being skeptical at first.

"What's the use of it and how you got it?" Probably, this was my final question on that encounter.

As he begins to disclose I came to know, where and why his parent got disappeared two weeks earlier? Actually, being out of concern Joshua's parent met a sage in order to know and secure the future of son as he was trying his level best to get a job but failing miserably. That Talisman was handed to Joshua's parent by the sage. It was insisted that tying that eternally to his neckline will soon ensure a good job and will wipe out all the worries, depression, anger and frustration of Joshua.

I'm not sure whether getting a job had anything to do with that talisman. But, when I recently met him he said how he got a job and got fired after six months. He was the same jobless standing in front of me when I met him the last time. Probably, more tortured and frustrated than before. I don't believe in things like a talisman can change one's future. And I also sturdily oppose the self proclaimed god man who promises to make over any one's future.

I'm conferring you my talisman and strongly recommending you to follow dos and don'ts for a long time jobless. Because, joblessness persisting for a long could prove some time fatal to someone. I call it as my talisman because unlike the talisman given to Joshua, this will be surely rewarding. Believe me. You can also take these suggestions as my mantras to fight the odds of joblessness and come across as a champion.

Your Invisible Enemy: Isolation

"Hello,

How are you brother?

How you called me?

I thought you have forgotten me or trying to part ways", these were my words as I received a call from my same master degree friend, Sandeep.

He laughed gently and replied, "Don't worry, I will never forget you, you are my brother and I have only love for you."

"Then, why you were not picking my calls or not making any call from yourself?", I asked in return.

I was guessing the reason to not picking call - A little bit confused as he was commenting and liking whatever I posted on my social account but reluctant to receive my calls.

"Actually, from quite a few days I have stopped receiving any one's call, neither friends nor family. Only talk to parent at times", Said Sandeep.

"Why so?", I questioned.

He replied, "Since, I'm jobless for so long, I feel humiliated whenever I find someone's call on my phone. I dreaded to receive a call as I have to face the very same question every time, Have you got any job? And I hate this question the most. So I choose to be happy all alone"

I settled with his reply as we were on same wavelength as far as those feeling were concerned.

He further added that he is planning to completely dump his social presence. I opposed this thought instantly.

"You are heading toward a self inflicted isolation, don't do this, It would be fatal to you," I asserted.

"Ok, brother", he responded (And then actual conversation progressed).

When you are jobless for a prolonged period, isolation does occur. Either society will isolate you or this could be done by yourself. Getting isolated will do nothing but break the bank of your worries, depression. Isolation deprives you of the chance to show your creativity, kill your skill and scrap any possible opportunities. You need to be involved with society, friends and family; you never know when an opportunity will knock your door in which appearance.

You could easily find how some of movie star accidently found their first role when they gambled their entire fortune and were staring down the barrel.

Once I read in one of the renowned newspaper how a 20 years old girl bagged a Tamil language film.

One day a Tamil movie's shooting was going on somewhere at interior location in Mumbai. As usual crowd stormed to that very place to experience the shoot of the film and witness the live encounter with movie stars.

Amid shooting director mesmerized by a face popping over from the crowd. He walked eagerly and called that girl in front and asked what your name is?

"Pooja (Name changed)", she replied.

"What's your age?", the director asked.

I'm 20 years of age and a graduate student originally from south but settled here in Mumbai for education.

Then the director explained, "You are very beautiful. And actually, I am looking for a face like you for my next movie."

"I want you to sign for my next two films if you wish", said the director.

"Yes, I would love to … but, I don't know Tamil language as well as acting," the girl replied.

"Don't worry, you will be trained for this for two months and will be provided other required support", director explained.

As it all got confirmed, the girl was smiling with glittery eyes. She was overjoyed to thank her fortune turner, the director.

Latter, she explained in an interview how it was difficult to believe on her fate and to make her parent believe that their daughter bagged two movies from nowhere. She revealed some day she had wished to modeling and try her luck in acting but, never thought that this will happen so ridiculously.

So, never isolate yourself. This could be a short term escape but will be a long term imprisonment because, isolation will only harm you nothing else.

You Are an Actor: Donning a Positive Outlook

I think we all are a born actor. Sometimes we showcase our acting talent so profoundly that people get deceived so easily. We transform our outlook without putting off costumes. We fake to appear which we are not from inside. Bearing a positive outlook all the time is not that difficult. Unleash your hidden actor and practice more of it. The key point is the fact that what we assume ourselves and try to appear will become a huge reality although we will be faking it.

Human and dog are the only creature in this world that reflects themselves same as what will be constantly inflicted on them, it doesn't matter its real or fake. For example if a person constantly bombarded with words like *"You are negative"* then after a certain time his thought, action, behavior will automatically begin to demonstrate negativity.

One day sitting at home, my father was in dismay, depressed, donning a dull face, eyes were red and tears were on way through his eyes. This was due to some serious tension; call it a business catastrophe mixed with family setbacks.

Amid all this someone knocked the door. My mother rushed to open. Next few moments what I witnessed surprised me a lot, I was awestruck.

As our guest was about to enter the room, I saw father immediately wiped up his tear and began the conversation with a normal outlook, a positive one. Further, conversation progressed and I saw a normal conversation transformed into a laughter riot. This particular happening left me spellbound. I wondered how someone could manage such a huge make over within such a short span of time.

Later, after guest's sendoff, I asked my father, "How you managed to transform your outlook so easily and successfully?"

"You are an actor," I said.

On a serious note, father replied, "my son! I too have learnt this courtesy some bitter experiences of my life. No one wants to talk to anyone who spread a sense of negativity and dullness. People will keep distant away from you if you are a complainer of circumstances, every one like to see a smiling face when they meet someone."

He further added, "When I used to blubber in front of other considering they will understand my problems and will extend a helping hand, my value deteriorated in the eye of those people, they started to make a distance from me, they made mockery of my compulsions. So, I stopped this practice and also suggest you the same. Never put forth your compulsions before anyone. Even if you are hurt from inside always don a positive outlook. Then only people will show importance and respect to you."

"Hmmm, I will practice it," I responded.

That particular lesson I learnt that day, I try my best to keep it in practice. Maintaining a positive outlook is necessary in job search. If you don't have positive appearance, your employer will misinterpret as if you are not confident enough. There will be a lack of determination in your words and this will go against you. You see everyone fear more or less facing an interview or a public speaking. But, smart people never let that fear to be apparent. They have mastered the art to maintain a positive appearance.

Practice to embrace a positive outlook will boost your self esteem and self confidence. This will facilitate you while approaching for a job interview. Positive outlook indirectly gifts a smiling face. We as human always gets attracted towards a good looking, positive and happy face. Besides these, this kind of outlook also proves handy in case of rejection. It will be a lot easier to scrub off rejection.

Extra Time: The time for wonders

I discussed it earlier in third part but, again just to remind you and stress little bit more on the value of leisure time here's this section. Being jobless you are gifted with one of the most precious gift in the world, the extra time. Many people want many out of his life but they can't as they are running out of time. They don't have time to try different things or to experiment with their present for a better future.

But you have all the time in the world to do any wonder. Don't waste your time on social media scrolling and reading random posts, sending tweets, gossiping and complaining. Go back on drawing board and find out your plan A, plan B, or Plan C if things not falling at place. Mark strategies and look to implement it. Small strategies and plan will be easy to execute and monitor. Take small steps and see if it is in right direction. Always harness your extra time in building and redefining yourself. It doesn't mean you have only to do out of the box; it could be anything like reading motivational books, working on any specific skill set, increasing your knowledge through books and videos, working on new projects, working on your health etc.

The point is that you must do all those possible things that will transform. You should feel more improved than the last day. People could easily notice that your growth is not stagnant.

How to use your extra time?

♣ Take a training and certification course.

♣ Spend quality time with yourself like Going for a walk or attending a public event. This will maximize your productivity while job search.

♣ Increasing your skills. Not necessarily related to your job search.

♣ Working on your fitness. Fitness exercise helps in bringing positivity and enhancing personal IQ.

♣ Join a temporary service either for free or for money. For example – free tutoring. The engaged mind will keep away negativity from your vicinity.

♣ Start volunteering other in their works. You should feel you are injured but not dead. You should be grateful for the fact that you are still useful to others even if you are jobless.

♣ Look for your hidden talent and begin polishing it. This may lead to an alternate career option.

Keeping The Eagle Eyes

I can understand that god has crafted each one of the creatures diversely but it's in our hand what we incorporate through learning from others. It could be a bird, an animal, an insects or a human every individual have some unique qualities that could be embraced by others.

When it comes to awareness and agility eagle is one such bird that strikes me first. Have you observed an eagle before? Eagle could easily trace an opportunity or a problem sitting high at distant. Their's agility is impeccable. Even sitting distant from their nest they are quite aware of all the happenings in their vicinity. They are hard to be deceived.

As a potential job searcher you must have the eagle eyes. If things not happening that easily the key is to keep your eyes wide open. The clouds of opportunities are always present there for you, it's your duty to identify and grab them. But sadly due to reasons like our dead attitude and confined vision we are not able to do so. But the real catch here is you can practice few steps to open up yourself to new opportunities and possibilities.

Ways to open yourself to new opportunities and possibilities

The Power of Visualization: Nature says what we visualize more often and frequently is directly to do with the happenings.

You got a dream. Practice visualizing your dream as reality. Always dress, behave, think and act accordingly. The more you practice more will be the certainty that every step of yours will be in the direction towards bringing that visualization to possibilities and that possibilities will lead to opportunities. Therefore, continue visualizing your dream even while you fall asleep.

Persist with Learning: Build and persist with learning attitude. Learn new things through videos, books or through internet. More you will add to your knowledge more understandings will come to you. And with more understandings come all the possibilities and opportunities that could exist under this galaxy. The persistence in learning will lead you to following:

- ℵ Find a new career path.
- ℵ Find new cause or purpose of life.
- ℵ Find new job, probably your dream job.
- ℵ The best of all you will have that confidence in your ability that whatever you learnt can be used to create opportunities for yourself as well as others.

Never Hold Yourself Back: No matter how hard the destiny hitting you never surrender to circumstances. Do whatever you want to do. Live your life to the fullest. Do experiments. Just give it a shot for which you are procrastinating. Restricting yourself means killing your inner artist at least what I perceive as. The Proclaimed author Wayne Dyer has to say related to restriction through his book *"Don't Die with Your Music Still in You" within you is person of unlimited possibilities, but restrictive thinking let that music out.*

Don't be Afraid to Take Risk: You may have came across Swami Vivekananda's saying

"Take risk, if you succeed you can lead and if you fail you can guide" It's wonderful you are in win-win situation the either way.

Still we are skeptical in taking risk. Playing it safe will let you go peacefully but this will be temporary. When you choose to play safe remember you are avoiding short term injuries or pain but you are missing something great that is adventures. Every new activity we perform has some hidden adventure. We should thrive on this. So, throw yourself at everything that you think of. Is this about starting a business, getting a degree, going on protest to support something, creating a video, writing a book or putting yourself on stage? Just go for it. I know that before you begin to act question of failure start haunting you. Sit relaxed and ask yourself what is the worst that could happen? That business would fail? What if your book doesn't sell? So what? You must accept the fact that what counts is adventure not the outcomes.

Don't be Judgmental: The ugly truth is when we judge someone; we don't define them, we define ourselves as judgmental people. We

should bring a halt on judging someone. The bottom line is when you look reluctant to accept anyone's lifestyle, beliefs you are actually closing your possibilities. For example
– let's imagine you are talking to someone who can help you to pull out you from whole job search process. But, you are showing disagreement and passing your judgment over their way of talking, appearance or ability then it's quite certain that vibrations of being judgmental will reach to them and they will stop even giving a second thought to your request. That person will drop his idea to help you. So, stop judging people and widen the corridor of possibilities.

Get Together with New Faces: Don't hesitate to meet new people. Get together whenever you get a chance. Be it a conference, a personal meeting or a public event. You never know how and in which way destiny having something for you. When you meet new faces what you may get are:

ℵ A support to your ideas of doing a business. Either collaboration with you or by just supporting you.

א A surprise calls offering you a job that may have a terrific position.

Travel to Explore: To explore the world of possibilities & opportunities you must initiate travelling. At first don't make this messy, travelling doesn't mean you should target a global tour, No, not at all. You could start with just moving from one corner to other in your vicinity or travel within your state.

As you will travel the window of possibilities will open. This universe will offer a lot in your plate. For instance – just search and wonder for a moment how many of today's young entrepreneurs make their career by opening the floodgate of possibilities just by travelling. Young entrepreneurship of Oyo Rooms is one such example. Idea to create an online platform for better room facility at lower prices punched his mind only when he travelled a lot and faced some difficulties with it. Remember a problem for other is an opportunity for someone.

What Did You Think of "*Congratulation! You Are Jobless*"?

First of all, thank you for purchasing this book **"Congratulation! You Are Jobless : Conquering The Unemployed Evil"**. *I know you could have picked any number of books to read, but you picked this book and for that I am extremely grateful.*

I hope that it added at value and quality to your everyday life & successfully generated a whole new thought process as potential jobless or jobseekers. If so, it would be really nice if you could share this book with your friends, family as well as any other who struggling his way through the unemployment phase – feeling depressed by posting to **Facebook***,* **Twitter & all other social media platforms or by mouth of words.**

If you enjoyed this book and found some benefit in reading this, I'd like to hear from you and hope that you could take some time to post a review on Amazon. Your feedback, suggestions for any changes or additions & support will help the author to greatly improve his writing craft for future projects and make this book even better.

You can follow this link to https://www.amazon.in/dp/B07694KGHF *now.*

I want you, the reader, to know that your review could be a make or break for an author who has put forth blood, sweats & tears of writing and publishing. Therefore, I request you to please be as honest as possible while posting your reviews. If you'd like to **leave a review**, *all you have to do is to go with over mentioned link and away you go. I love you as my reader & always will be also I wish you all the best in your future success!*